Our culture is chang  church planting and The need for fresh expressions of the church to be pioneered is well documented, yet so few seem to be taking on this new adventure. I'm convinced after reading this beautiful little book that it's because we're having the wrong conversations around calling and vocation. Through storytelling and personal experience, Sean probes into the "why" that drives church planters and forces the reader to sit with questions that rarely get asked. I think every church planter, whether in a traditional paradigm or a bi-vocational one, needs to read this book.

Drew Thurman
Church Planter at Renaissance .
Hub Director for Forge Boston

The Adventure of Vocation is an exciting road map for those seeking to understanding their calling while thoughtfully engaging the art of church planting in our post-Christian culture.

Daniel McIntosh
Parish Network; Church Planter

While *The Adventure of Vocation: Exploring the Contours of Calling, Identity, and Place* is set in the context of ministry and particularly in the context of church planting, Sean provides any reader an opportunity to consider the calling God has in order to find fulfillment as a person and as a servant of God. It's appropriate to have "Adventure" in the title because Sean leads the reader on a journey of discovery. His narrative style weaves his own story with solid principles and challenges for the reader to consider. This is an engaging book that will lead people to thoughtfully and individually listen to where God's Spirit is leading.

Bob Ransom
Director of Generate

We know what roams the dark parking lots of the 21st Century—vampires and zombies. I am personally in need of writers unafraid to shine a light. Or even better, show up with a wooden stake and some holy water. Sean shows real guts in his latest book. He shares the raw details of his story. Then, he takes the stake of vocation, with his struggles as hammer, and pounds a hole in the decaying heart of American church-planting practice. Am I being overly dramatic? Maybe. But there are moments when it feels post-apocalyptic out here. I'm talking about the state of our own thinking and less about the culture. The first step in any journey of integrity is to tell ourselves the truth, to map the contours of a new terrain. If there is ever a "how-to" guide written by Sean, I would gladly carry it in my back pocket like a spray-bottle of holy water. Until then, *The Adventure of Vocation* will have to do. I just wish it was heftier, you know, for the inevitable face-offs with church-planting vampires.

Dust Kunkel
Executive Coach/Leadership Development
Northwest District LCMS

I enjoyed reading Sean's latest book on calling. He does a wonderful job weaving his story with thoughtful, reflective questions. I would recommend anyone praying about church planting or vocational change to pick this up and give it a read. Thanks Sean for letting us see and learn from your journey.

Charles Campbell
Director, Send Network Planter Training

Three years ago I planted a church in Portland, Oregon and nothing really went according to plan. The melee of church planting left me and my team in a sort of identity crisis wondering where God was and if we were really called to be church planters in the first place. My walk with God has deepened and books like this one have been a lifeline for me as I lead our team through the gauntlet of exploring how to both seek the welfare of the city, and minister saving grace, by starting things we can be passionate about that will give us the sustainability we need to make a long lasting impact.

Sam Wake
Social Entrepreneur & Pastor of Movement Portland

THE ADVENTURE OF VOCATION

SEAN BENESH

The Adventure of Vocation: Exploring the Contours of Calling, Identity, and Place

Published by Intrepid. www.intrepidmissions.com

The mission of Intrepid is to elevate marginalized communities and people through training church planters, pastors, and missionaries to start social enterprises to sustain themselves long-term so they can seek the betterment of these overlooked and neglected places and people as they start new churches, businesses, and non-profits.

Intrepid
2034 NE 40th Ave. #414
Portland, OR 97212

Manufactured in the United States of America.

ISBN: 978-0-578-23154-9

Contents

FOREWORD

Daniel Yang

I suspect the reason why Sean asked me to write the foreword to *The Adventure of Vocation* has something to do with my experience and research in church planting in North America. However, what he probably didn't know, until the reading of this foreword, is that I found his book to be relevant not mainly because of my work but because I'm a normal dad raising five children.

My eldest three are teenage boys, and when they aren't playing video games or on the phone with someone (of the female persuasion!) or hustling a deal online trying to save and make a dollar, they're learning to be young adults who want to do something significant with their lives. I pray all of them would be life-long followers of Jesus, involved in church planting and other missional ventures. However, I worry sometimes that because I was a vocational church planter, my kids will intentionally avoid that path. I'm not sure, but I support them whether or not they do. But I do know from my work in studying culture, denominations, and networks that a large part of the future of church planting in North America depends on my kids and their generation seeing the connection between vocation and mission.

We are currently raising the largest generational cohort that America has ever seen. And in the last few years, they began entering colleges and universities for the first time, many of which were designed for an industrial model of work that's quickly disappearing. Moreover, for those in this generation that grew up in church, they're learning about mission in a time when much of the European models of missional engagement adapted into the North American context are being challenged in many cases, and altogether abandoned in others.

Both our economic and missional models of vocation feel like Saul's armor to this emerging generation of young adults.

This is why I appreciate Sean's voice and his framing of vocation as an adventure and church planting as much more than launching weekend services. Sean has lived and done ministry in a part of North America–the Pacific Northwest–where people understand most the "start-up" culture and the value of an individual's contribution. This is the leading edge of platform networks and an information-based economy. And it could also be the leading edge of mission in North America.

By framing the seed of church planting as current needs + who you are + Missio Dei, Sean is taking seriously that anyone and everyone with the Holy Spirit can be a church planter. This does not lessen the importance of community and church leadership. Rather, it takes the missional nature of the priesthood of all believers more seriously than the best practices of yesteryear. And it also takes seriously the fact that churches and church planting networks today are mobilizing only a small portion of the Body of Christ into mission.

So I join Sean in calling this generation and the next to embrace vocation as a part of the mission of God. The harvest is plentiful and it's time to better recognize how God is sending workers out through their vocation.

Daniel Yang

Director of the Send Institute at the Billy Graham Center of Wheaton College

INTRODUCTION

Why This Conversation Matters

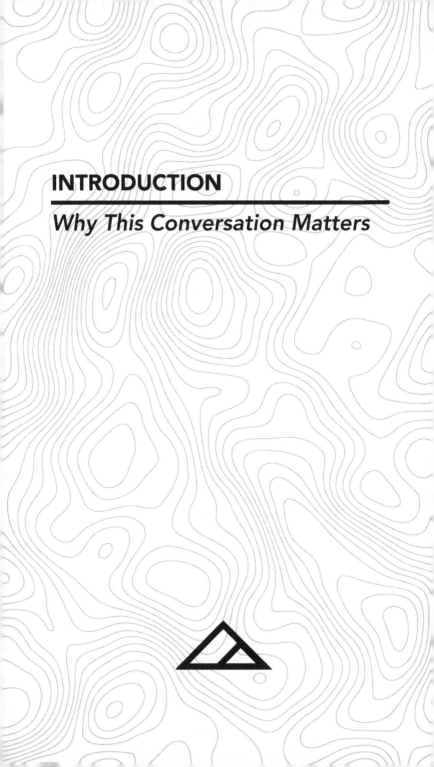

We long for meaning. We pursue it in the form of relationships, educational opportunities, career aspirations, family, experiences, and more. Whether we're conscious of it or not, this longing is what drives us. It is subterranean. We know it and feel it but are not always cognizant of its presence.

Why do we want a larger social media presence? Answer: To be known. Liked. Respected. What drives us as students? Answer: To earn the degree that will unlock the career path we hope and assume will bring us fulfillment. If you think of this as some shallow pursuit only adults experience then we fail to realize these longings are with us from the very beginning.

Children are great examples. They are unfiltered. When we ask them what they want to do or be when you grow up, their answers usually have to do with doing something meaningful and helping others. Kids are not thinking about accumulating possessions, cool Instagram-worthy vacations, or titles. Their focus is on a life of meaning (helping others) and doing something that they're interested in.

But then they grow up. They become like us.

Somewhere along the way we shift from doing something of significance to doing something that makes us money. Of course, we need money to live and survive in this world. However, for many of us altruism is shown the door and seemingly our own prestige, platform, and craving for accolades become our top motivators. Those longings and interests we held in our childhood have been set aside. Suppressed.

Yes, we all had far-flung ideas and crazy career aspirations as children. I'm not talking as much about the specifics ... astronaut, firefighter, NASCAR racer, POTUS, etc. Instead, I'm talking about what gives us meaning. It is at this point that thoughts about calling and vocation enter in.

They sit at the table waiting patiently to be invited into the conversation. They listen intently as we talk to other conversation partners about our life (titles, accolades, possessions, etc.). Never demanding attention, it is easy to forget they are there. Waiting. When the lights go out and our other dinner guests leave, calling and vocation are still at the table. Waiting.

Are calling and vocation simply religious niceties to appease a guilty conscious as we live under the weight of various obligations? How do we reclaim a sense of calling and vocation in the midst of a society which continues to distance itself from institutional Christianity (and rightly so)? More specifically, what and how does calling shape the conversation of church planting? In particular, influencing where we plant churches and even why.

Why is this conversation important for planting churches today? Why is this important for missions, starting businesses, launching non-profits, and the like? Because many of us have wrapped our identity into *what* we do ... and *where*. There's an enormous disparity in the places where churches and startups are being launched. In our pursuit of meaning and taking our cues from culture, we have inadvertently turned church planting and launching startups into curated and appealing images on social media. Trendy and beautiful people. Beautiful and appealing places. And of course, we need to use the correct presets and filters on our photos in order to show them in just the right light.

Is that what ministry has turned into?

This book digs into this very conversation. Don't worry. While I strive to be honest I'm not standing from afar lobbing accusatory stones at you. Instead, I'm with you. I struggle with you. I strive to be honest and vulnerable which is risky. It just might dampen my own self-image.

I invite you into this journey of calling and vocation. I believe that we need to continue to wrestle through these conversations as we contemplate where and why we plant churches and launch startups, whether businesses or non-profits. We'll also explore related topics such as identity, place, and ultimately learning how to discern God's voice in all of this.

I've written somewhere close to fifteen books now. Every author weaves different themes throughout their writings. Sometimes it takes a while to notice them. These are born out of who are our, our leanings, curiosities and struggles, how we see the world. I realized that a certain theme had wormed its way in most of my writings. It is this very conversation . . . calling and vocation.

What you have before you are these disparate pieces extracted from various writings and collected into one book ... adapted, polished, and presented as a collective whole. Thank you for journeying with me on this adventure. I wish I could say it is all neat and tidy. It's not. My own failures and shortcomings prove that.

I invite you to dive deeper into this conversation.

CHAPTER 1

Calling, Vocation and Making Decisions

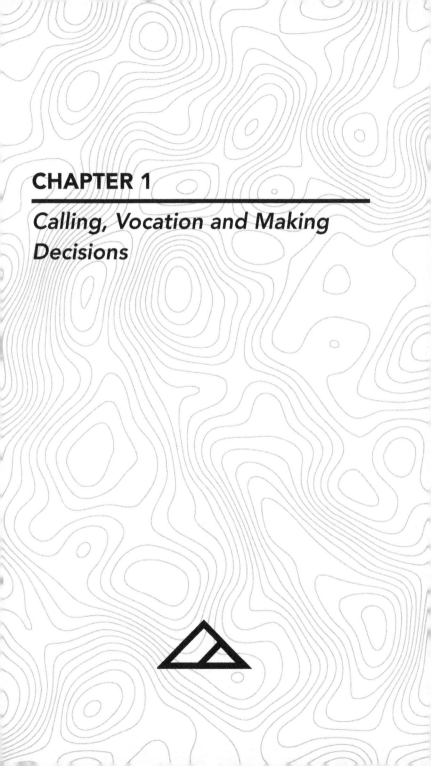

I am obsessed with motives—the "why" questions. As a fan of history I'm always interested in why certain places were settled, what went into the decision-making process, and the like. Over the past number of years, I had taught a course on the history of American cities. Part of our time was also spent uncovering the history of Portland.

Interestingly, Portland had shaky origins. It was one of numerous other communities along the Willamette and Columbia rivers that were popping up in the first half of the nineteenth century. Forests were cleared, land was sold, and people started moving in. Carving new communities out of nothing. In their haste the tree stumps were not even removed. That is how Portland become known as "Stumptown."

Each of these communities were competing with each other ... Portland, Oregon City, Linnton, St Helens, and more. But out of all of them, why did Portland alone become a city of note?

Such "why" questions are critical and deserve an answer.

As a former church planting strategist who was at the time working on a doctorate I was asking a lot of why questions in regards to church planting and where new churches were cropping up. Why? Why *there*? Why *not* there? Today I'm still probing for answers. Why questions matter.

Why do we decide to plant churches where we do? How could I leverage my research opportunities to find out more? I found that uncovering the why ... the motives of church planters ... is a tough hill to climb. And if I have difficulty dissecting my own motives I have a hunch that many other church planters are in the same boat.

One of the difficulties in conducting any type of research is moving away from the hard data toward that which is more subjective. In researching church planting across metro areas it is easy to determine where churches are being planted by simply locating their meeting places and plotting them on a map. It is cut-and-dry for the most part. It may not tell the entire story but at least it begins to come together.

However, I wanted to get into why church planters decided to plant where they did. That gets into calling. It takes an enormous amount of introspection and self-awareness to be able to wade through all of the motives that go into site selection. It is more than a conversation about geography; it is also a conversation about calling.

I recall the period in my life nearly two decades ago when I was on the front end of the journey of planting my first church. I can attest to the difficulty of choosing where exactly to do so. The best way for me to illustrate the difficulty is to draw back the curtain and let you into my own decision-making process. In many ways it was a messy and painstaking process with no normative template for everyone to follow. My hope in sharing this is that my own understandings, fumblings, and methods may shed light on how difficult the process can be.

The first time I helped plant a church was in Arizona. I vividly remember driving into Tucson with two other friends who were praying through whether to join me or not. I was living in California at the time but was on a trip to New Mexico interviewing about the possibility of a staff position at a church outside of Albuquerque. I extended my trip so I could visit Tucson where we were all exploring a church planting possibility.

I drove from Albuquerque to Phoenix where I picked these friends up from the airport and set off for Tucson. But I am already getting ahead of myself. How did I even narrow my own site selection down to Tucson of all places? Did I have a map up and simply threw darts at it? I suppose if I had a good aim I would have ended up planting in Hawai'i.

Surprisingly, it wasn't that difficult of a decision. My family and I had lived in Phoenix for several years while I was on staff at a church and attending seminary. My wife was originally from the Southwest and we both had family in Arizona, New Mexico, and Nevada. Apart from where I grew up in Iowa, it was the most familiar part of the country for me. At the time, we were in northern California, and when we talked about church planting we had made the decision to go back to the Southwest, to the desert. It was not necessarily even a spiritual decision. We wanted to be back closer to family and in an environment that we were familiar with.

Step one was selecting the region. Once we narrowed it down to the Southwest we began to prayerfully explore options focusing on Albuquerque, Phoenix, and Tucson.

Step two was choosing a city. We favored the larger ones over the smaller ones like Flagstaff, Las Cruces, Santa Fe, and so on.

Through networking I connected with a church planting strategist in Tucson. From the very first conversation we had on the phone it felt like something resonated. He answered my questions, told me about the vision his network of churches had for Tucson, and even encouraged me in the ideas I had on church planting at the time. After more conversations and emails over the ensuing weeks I planned a visit to Tucson in conjunction with my trip to Albuquerque. Church planting was enticing and I did not know whether to do so now or later. At the same time, I was exploring going on staff at a church near Albuquerque. Which brings us back to where I started this story.

While I had only been to Tucson once before it was still a familiar setting being in the Southwest. As the three of us drove from Phoenix to Tucson, we talked and prayed asking God to show us what he wanted and for clarity. We arrived in Tucson and made our way across the city to our hotel.

If first impressions were foundational for making decisions we would have turned the car around and drove back to Phoenix. We did not like what we saw of the city. There was no positive vibe or warm feelings that made us say, "Eureka! I found it!" By the time we arrived at the hotel we were dismayed and already questioning why we came. There was this sick feeling in my gut and I did not know what it meant. Was this God? Was it simply my unreliable emotions? Bad food? Were these feelings based upon my expectations of the built environment of the city? While I was familiar with Phoenix, and even though Tucson is only an hour and a half away, they are completely different cities. Was I feeling this way because I was simply overly tired from the travel? What was going on?

The church planting strategist met us at the hotel, and after some initial time chatting we set out to explore the city. Based upon who we were and the needs of the city he took us to a few places which he thought would be a good fit for us to plant a church. He talked about Tucson and the need for church planting across the city. The first site he took us to did not resonate at all. We did not "feel" anything and culturally it was not a fit. We simply did not like it. What was it that we did not like? I do not know if I could pinpoint that even now but we felt and experienced nothing. However, that was all about to change.

He took us to another site that he said he had been praying over for quite some time pleading with the Lord to send church planters there. As we crested the hill overlooking the area just as he was telling the story we had that "Eureka" moment.

That moment felt kind of odd on further consideration. How can it be quantified or measured? In working with church planters I've seen this happen over and over again. Sometimes it is powerful and intense while other times it is more subtle, like unfolding a map. I would tell planters that it is also like looking at something that's out of focus and that over time the picture becomes clearer. My experience seemed to be pretty quick and intense.

Now, what was that? Emotions? God? God working through my emotions? I am not too sure but my thinking and feelings moved quickly from not wanting to be in Tucson to all of a sudden sensing that this was all that I wanted. I could envision myself living there and planting a church. As we explored the area I became even more excited. Looking back, I wonder why I was excited and what resonated. We went house-hunting with the strategist and walked in and out of a number of model homes. I liked what I saw. We were no longer in

Tucson but in an edge-of-the-city suburb. It felt like home and was even familiar to where we lived in suburban Phoenix. Needless to say, we went for it. Several months later we made the move and began the church planting journey in that Tucson suburb.

Hindsight is always 20/20. Navigating God's will is indeed a tricky experience for us. Our theological backgrounds and underpinnings influence us greatly. For some it is a highly rationalistic process while for others it is strictly emotional. For me, it was somewhere in the middle. At that point in my life, I still had an aversion to cities and so the closest I could handle was, indeed, a suburb. Urban life still scared me, which explains why I felt angst driving across the city and staying at a hotel there.

Once I got out to the suburbs I felt I could breathe. Whatever took place was enough to get us to clean out our savings account and move to this new city. What was interesting was that after we launched we ended up moving the church out of that suburb. We had aspirations of planting a church for suburban families but most of those who came were college students. That began a slow migration. The church eventually moved from suburban to just a few blocks from the downtown business district and a few blocks in the other direction from the University of Arizona. I still scratch my head when I think about it.

As Christians, the decision making process, not only for church planting but for life decisions as well, becomes more complex in some ways because there is a critical factor in the equation—God. On the surface it might seem that having God in the picture should make the process easier, but in many ways our desire to follow him in obedience causes us to scrutinize the details all the more.

How exactly do we make decisions? Is it weighing the bottom line factors like what option will pay us the most? Which is the best career move? What kind of place will make me and my spouse happy? Which city has the best career or educational opportunities? What place makes us feel alive? Where is the greatest need (both real and perceived)? What is good for my family? Are we staying close to family or moving away from family? Do we stay in the area close to where we grew up or do we relocate to a different region or even another country? On top of that we always ask: What does God want for my life? There are numerous ideas and theories about determining God's will. How do we decide and what guides our thinking?

These are crucial questions when it comes to site selection for church planting. It goes beyond simply emotions or crunching numbers. Some argue that we ought to make decisions based upon what we see in Scripture. It seems as though we cannot do anything unless we feel "called" by God whether that involves sitting on some obscure church committee to deciding whether to pray for someone regularly or not. We end up reading our current theological assumptions back into Scripture.

The reality is what we assume is normative cannot be found in Scripture. We fail to realize that the Bible is a collection of God's revelation to mankind that spanned thousands of years. In that time frame empires rose and fell, numerous cities went from their apexes to becoming wastelands, and countless numbers of people who loved and worshiped God lived and died. Yes, God communicated directly and audibly to many, but again, it was over thousands of years and to only a select few. Given the scope of Scripture and the multitude of people who worshipped God an audible divine calling was not normative.

Most of us cannot claim God has spoken to us audibly. I am not here to enter into a debate about signs, wonders, cessation of gifts, and so on. What I am trying to communicate is this: most often when it comes to making decisions, both major and small, we most often do not hear God's audible words on the subject. If we did, we would not have to talk about motives and the issue would simply become about obedience.

If we do not hear God's audible voice then how do we choose where to plant a church? While God's audible voice may not be normative for most aspiring church planters, there still has to be a way to discern God's will and leadership in our lives. The tricky part comes when we attempt to reduce it to an equation or an exercise in logic and preference. On this issue I speak out of both sides of my mouth. On one hand I believe that listening for God's leading is an intuitive process. But that does not rule out weighing other factors like gifting, background and upbringing, preferences, geography, and simply what resonates.

I think back to my college days, sitting in a class taught by Dr. Stanley Udd at Grace University in Omaha, Nebraska. The course was on the Minor Prophets and I knew I was in over my head. I honestly do not remember anything from the class apart from two things. The first one was that in my final paper I completely botched my interpretation of the book of Zechariah. But Dr. Udd liked my drawing for the cover and had mercy on me. The second thing had nothing to do with the class.

I do not remember how the conversation came up but we got into a discussion concerning God's will and answered prayer. At that point, I had been a Christian for about four years and was still soaking everything in. Dr. Udd said something that has stuck with me to this day. He said that if we really want to know whether God is answering our prayers and leading us, then we simply pray with clear specifics but tell no one. He said that when we pray and then tell others about it, sometimes Christians on their own can make it happen. I understand as the Body of Christ we are to rally around and help one another, but we dare not miss his point. *When we petition God with clear specifics and he answers in the affirmative, there is no debate as to what has happened.* When I graduated not too long after that I decided to put his idea to the test.

After college we made the decision to move to Phoenix where I would begin seminary. In light of what Dr. Udd talked about, I created a list of very specific things that I began to bring before the Lord on a daily basis. I prayed ...

- for very affordable housing,
- for our moving expenses to be covered,
- for me to find a staff position at a church as a youth pastor,
- for a car with air conditioning since we were moving to Arizona,
- and for help with seminary tuition.

It was definitely a tall order but what did I have to lose? My desire was simply to know that God was in this with us, but I was not prepared for what would happen next.

After praying several months all of these prayer requests were specifically and fully answered in a two-week span. I was utterly shocked, amazed, humbled, and deeply grateful. Out of the blue I contacted a church about a youth ministry opportunity not knowing whether they even had a youth pastor or was looking. There was no ad or job posting that I answered but I got a Phoenix area phone book, found their address, and sent them my resume. The pastor called me immediately. I found out their youth pastor had just resigned. They saw my resume and knew it was from the Lord. I flew out, interviewed, and they voted to hire me all in the same visit. Just wait, it gets better! They told me they were going to pay our moving expenses, too.

We had family in the area at the time. They had a house there plus one in Mexico and were building another in Colorado. Their house in the Phoenix area was vacant and fully furnished. They had asked us if we would stay there for free and that they would cover all the utilities. Not only that, but they had a car in the garage they needed us to drive on occasion to make sure it continued to run well—and it had air conditioning! Free house, car with AC, free utilities, and even a credit card to help us take care of the house.

Did I mention that out of the entire Phoenix metropolitan area, which is an enormous sprawling city, the house we were moving into was less than two miles from the church? Oh, and it had a pool. Lastly, I applied at the seminary and received a scholarship for half of my tuition. I learned a lot about prayer and God's will from that experience.

Is that then the normative way we are to make decisions? I had opportunities to go to seminary elsewhere but opted not to. It wasn't even much of a decision. Phoenix or Dallas? Phoenix won hands down. Are we to believe that in the decision-making process God also utilizes our interests and desires?

Why was Phoenix even a possibility? Because we had family there and we had been there before. My wife was born in Albuquerque and moved to Iowa in the third grade but had come back to Albuquerque and Phoenix every summer since then. I first visited Phoenix as a child as my grandparents had retired there. My mom also lived there for a short while before she got married to my dad.

Those experiences were formative. It's as though we couldn't shake them. Even after ten years of living in the Pacific Northwest the desert Southwest has a magnetic pull on us. I'm sure it'll only be a matter of time before we transition back. So how did we end up in Portland and the Northwest?

CHAPTER 2

Discerning Signs Along the Way

People have different ways of making decisions. The processes we follow are influenced by our upbringing, temperament, personality, and theological leaning. I've been sharing my own experiences of how I made and currently make decisions. In this chapter I will share more. Looking back, I cannot say I have a well-defined pattern or routine of making major life decisions, particularly when it comes to ministry. Maybe, because it *is* ministry I feel I am not required to follow the same line of reasoning if I were applying for another job in a different career path … salary, benefits, opportunities for advancement, etc. Instead, I have oftentimes taken pay cuts so I could be part of a particular ministry and have done so gladly.

The second story I would like to share concerns our second church planting experience in the Pacific Northwest. The factors surrounding this decision were much different from any other we have made to date. As before, part of the process was highly emotive. But it also involved a thorough investigation of me as a candidate. Sometimes self-disclosure can be frightening. Not surprisingly, we like to share whatever casts us in a good light. We have a self-image or persona to uphold and we share or reveal only our "acceptable flaws." It is akin to sitting in an interview and the interviewer asks about our weaknesses. If we have a problem with lateness, we are not going to volunteer that and instead go with something safe. It is not that I am ashamed of how I made decisions, but they become highly personal experiences that we cannot detach ourselves from. In fact, it is exactly these experiences that form and shape us. So how did we end up back in the whirlwind of church planting in Vancouver, British Columbia?

The genesis of the story dates back to 1997 when I was still in college. There was always a steady stream of ministries and missions organizations that came through to try to recruit students. Some were local, others were national, and many were international in focus. Needless to say, we had a high exposure to what God was doing globally.

During one chapel meeting, an alum spoke about camp ministry up in Southeast Alaska. It sounded so exciting and appealing that my wife Katie and I came back to hear more during an evening information meeting. As we continued to learn about the ministry and hear of the needs I turned to Katie and we both said, "Why not?" I cannot say there was much or really any prayer involved other than we saw a need and decided to jump in to help. That one decision set us on a trajectory that we are still on today ... literally.

On a side note, sometimes I believe we spend too much time pondering and praying instead of simply doing. I know that might sound almost heretical but I do not believe everything we do needs a special prior calling. What would happen if more people simply rolled up their sleeves and jumped at the chance of missionary engagement?

We continued to make plans and preparations for our summer in Alaska as camp counselors. We raised our funds, bought our plane tickets, and after graduation flew up to Juneau. While the season of ministry was exciting as we saw God work and move, it was what happened on the final day as we drove into town to get on the plane bound for home that changed everything.

The camp experience was amazing and it opened our eyes to the Pacific Northwest. We fell in love with the area. I was beginning to get into the whole outdoorsy thing as our camp sat right on a pristine beach tucked in a bay on the Inside Passage surrounded by snow-capped mountains and glacier-fed rivers. I loved the wilderness.

Wildlife was everywhere, ranging from whales to sea lions to bears to bald eagles. Some of the camp staff had even shot a bear in the camp so I ate bear sausage for the first time, along with other nearby delicacies including fresh crab and halibut. But I never saw an actual live bear. Despite all of our treks into the forest and clambering up and down mountains I had not seen a single one. There were lots of scat but no bear. I had lived in the Alaskan boonies for three months. It was now our last day and I desperately wanted to see a bear. I was also wrestling with calling. I had just graduated from college and was wondering what was next. God stirred something in our hearts.

The journey back to Juneau was like a funeral procession. I did not want to leave. I did not want to head back to the Midwest. The thought of trading in snow-capped mountains and the ocean for soy bean fields and cattle pastures was nauseating. As we were on the boat riding along the edge of the bay to where the van waited for us I began praying, "Lord, I want to come back. I love the Pacific Northwest."

I then stopped and thought about how I would even know whether or not God wanted me to come back. We wanted to come back. We loved the region. I then prayed, "Lord, I know this is silly, but I have not seen a bear the whole time here. If you show me a brown bear on the way back I know this will be a sign that you want us to come back." I quickly put that prayer out of my mind because I thought it was a bit childish.

We made it around the bay into the cove to the pick-up point. We loaded our luggage and began the somber drive to Juneau. We were about 40 miles north of the city. About half way back I happened to glance out my window ... and saw a brown bear just standing by the side of the road. In my haste I told the driver to stop the van and I jumped out. I stood in bewildered amazement and excitement as I watched the bear lumber across the road. I was speechless.

In our sophisticated spirituality it is easy to begin explaining away our unexplainable experiences. We are raised culturally, even as Christians, to be highly rationalistic and logical. We are products of Modernity. And so, in this moment, I asked myself: Was God responsible for showing me the brown bear? Come on, there are bears *everywhere* in Alaska. This was merely a coincidence. How can I make a major life decision based upon seeing a furry four-legged animal? Since that fateful day that bear has haunted my mind. I kept asking myself what it meant. Were we to go back to that camp in Alaska to do ministry? Or was there something more?

That experience opened up my eyes and heart to the Pacific Northwest. I began exploring and seeking out what God had in mind for us there. Was the bear sighting really a coincidence? Even though in less than a year we moved to Arizona, which is about as far as one can get from the Pacific Northwest, the bear experience never left me. Over the years it began intensifying in ways that I cannot describe.

Yes, we moved to Phoenix which I believe God had clearly led us to do. Yes, we planted a church in Tucson which I believe God had also led us to do. When I became a church planting strategist in Tucson, it was evidently clear that this was what God was leading me to do. By that point eight years had elapsed since the bear-spotting event in Alaska but it was still fresh in my mind and still haunted my thoughts.

A year after I became a strategist, my yearning to get back to the Northwest kept growing. I made trips to Seattle and Portland and every time I was there I felt at home like never before. The smells of the ocean and the trees, as well as the wetter climate, reminded me of Alaska. When I decided to pursue a doctorate there was only one city I looked at:

Seattle. The brown bear was even influencing where I pursued my studies!

I began studying the different Northwest cities from afar, and for various reasons I was making numerous trips up to the area whether for school or training events for our Tucson church planters. During this time, I explored numerous ministry opportunities in Seattle, Portland, and even down to San Francisco.

One of the initial courses I took for my doctorate lasted for two weeks in Seattle. Since the focus of my program was on global urban contexts, we spent much time learning about and discussing cities. During one of his lectures Ray Bakke referred to Vancouver, BC. He explained how in many ways it was a model city with its ethnic diversity, distinct neighborhoods, and lack of freeways. I was mesmerized and knew I had to explore this city that was just up the road and across the 49th Parallel from Seattle.

On a free weekend I decided to drive north. I had no idea where I would stay and had only one name as a contact person who was a fellow church planting strategist in Vancouver. Upon arriving I was utterly amazed. It was a completely different world and the city was unlike anything I had ever seen or experienced. I did a whirlwind tour of the city and explored as much as my time allowed including a quick jaunt up to Whistler. Vancouver is a different city. I was not prepared for the enormous differences between it and Seattle, in terms of its built environment and its sheer diversity. Vancouver perplexed me.

I filed away this experience in my thinking about the future. Over the ensuing years opportunities would come and go in the Northwest but nothing quite grabbed me. There were also several false starts in our attempt to move to the Northwest, whether in church planting or as a strategist. I began wondering if the brown bear was simply the experience of a young believer at a vulnerable and impressionable time in his life. But the more I tried to dismiss it the more unsettled I felt. The pull was strong. At the same time, we had sold our home and begun building a new house south of Tucson. In many ways it was a dream home; it was large with more than enough room for our family. We saw it as a place where we could stay for the rest of our lives.

But something happened. I could not go through with it. Three weeks before we were to move in we backed out and were able to get our money back.

I decided to take a new ministry opportunity in Illinois. It seemed like a logical move on many fronts as it was a step up the denominational food chain with better money and an increase in ministry responsibility. I would oversee all of the campus ministries statewide, as well as church planting for the 35 and under crowd. There was already an amazing team in place and my supervisor was a friend. The move also meant we would be close to family for the first time in ten years and our boys could grow up knowing grandparents.

My dad had recently died and it would give us a chance to be close to my mom. In every way it seemed a great move; it was fiscally sound, and a smart career choice. But I was miserable.

On the first day of the job I walked into my new office with my new laptop and phone on my desk waiting for me. I sat down in my chair with my newly pressed dress slacks and shiny shoes. In Tucson as a strategist I was a shorts and flip-flops guy. As I looked around the room I almost started to cry. What did I just do? Instantly it became like a nightmare from which I could not wake up. It had nothing to do with the people around me who were top notch and great.

I felt like a fish out of water. The brown bear was almost roaring at me now. Did I just make the biggest mistake of my life? It was early November and by December I had cut out a picture of Vancouver and stuck it on our refrigerator at home. I was in a funk, the boys hated their new school and living in Illinois, and our house gave us the creeps.

Not too long after that I was in Atlanta for a series of meetings for workers from across North America who oversee church planting. While there, I knew I had to reconnect with the church planting strategist from Vancouver. We set up a time to meet for breakfast. The night before, as I talked with Katie on the phone, she felt impressed to tell me what she had learned that day from her time with God. She had felt that God had told her to tell me that wherever we went I had her full support. She knew I was miserable. We had talked about Vancouver. But how could we move there? We had just moved to Illinois, our kids were still adjusting to their new school, city, and state, and we were close to family. What would they think if we up and left again? Why would I walk away from all of that and take a leap of faith to plant a church from scratch in a new city and country? As we talked on the phone I said, "We have to go for it. I can no longer ignore that brown bear. I have to know if seeing it was indeed from the

Lord or not. I do not care if we fail miserably. We need to respond in obedience."

To say it was a leap of faith seems now like an understatement. It was a complete free fall. I resigned from a great ministry job, sold a lot of stuff, including one of our vehicles, and moved in with my mom during transition. We had no supporters, whether individuals or churches. Slowly, one came onboard and so did our denomination, but when we set the date to move we had no idea how we would do it. We began praying for $10,000 for moving and settling-in expenses. Miraculously, our needs were soon met.

We drove across the country in a lumbering moving truck, not knowing where we would live or even how much it would take to live in one of the most expensive cities in the world. There were many times on the long stretches of highway where I was in tears praying and wondering what in the world I had just done. Driving across the endless sand hills of western Nebraska, the expanses of northern Utah and southern Idaho, all I had were my thoughts, God's presence, our two boys in the cab of the truck with me, and a myriad of country western music stations. I felt like we were just entering the gauntlet.

The truck we rented was complete junk and had more issues than a guest on Dr. Phil. We lost half our mattresses, a dresser, and some other furniture from water damage which our insurance refused to cover. Our car was broken into the first week in Vancouver, only to be broken into again three months later. It finally died on us. And not having the resources to fix it or even insure it we become dependent upon public transit. Katie's health took a serious hit and she had been hospitalized several times.

One bad thing after another seemingly came our way. It was simply a challenge to live, let alone to think about church planting. But we were there. We made it. We were alive. God is good. He had a plan. We were humbled to simply follow him and attempt to plant a church there. We loved it there. Our boys blossomed. Our walk with God deepened. We saw him work and move in ways that surpassed logic. He was (and is) with us.

Deciding where to plant a church is no small feat. At times it seems like a logical and rational decision. I have seen guys take a very methodical approach whereby they base the location on research, how well their personalities and the needs of a particular community match up. On the other hand, I have seen guys who make their decision based wholly on visions from God.

As a church planting researcher, I know that studying the motivating factors behind site selection can become problematic. What criteria should be used? How do I navigate between those who take a methodical approach versus those who rely on God's promptings? Oftentimes I liken God's calling or will to an airplane's black box. If the plane should crash and burn, somehow that box survives always intact. It makes one wonder why the whole plane was not made out of that same indestructible material. For church planters, that black box is our calling. When everything else crashes and burns, it alone remains to keep us going.

But taken too far, I think our callings can become off limits: Do Not Touch! All we have to do is invoke "God's call" to stop anyone who questions whatever we are doing. It is not for me to judge or be disrespectful of someone's calling. Instead, I simply want to ask whether or not we are hearing God clearly or if we even understand the scope of God's will for us in a specific situation. Is it God's will that a city's hip and trendy districts and the well-to-do white suburbs receive more church planters while the broken, neglected, and ethnically diverse parts of the city remain under-churched?

One area of interest when studying the geography of church planting is to figure out why churches were planted in their specific locations. What were the determining factors that led church planters to decide where to start a church? Was it a matter of personal preference? Did their church planting network or denomination steer them in a certain direction? Was it based upon need, such as the lack of churches in a particular community or in an area in economic decline in need of hope? Or was it out of familiarity with a certain location or the people among whom they were planting?

CHAPTER 3

The Geography of Calling and Finding a Fit

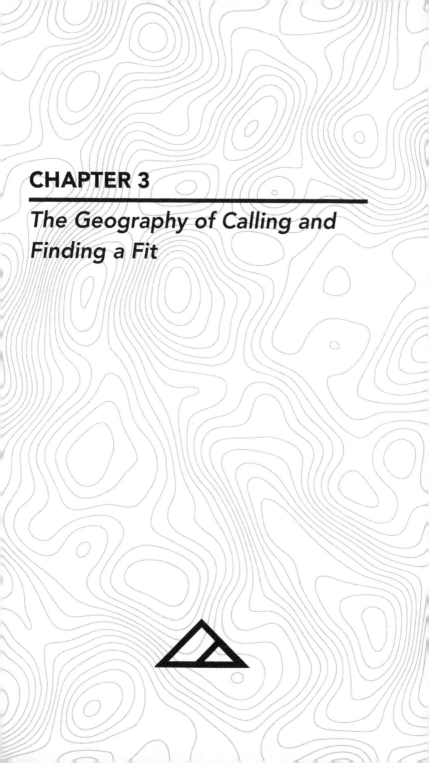

Determining God's calling can indeed be tricky. It is highly subjective and especially is personal and spiritual. There are no templates for figuring out God's will since he communicates to us in myriad ways. No two individual's stories are alike. I look back on my experiences in church planting and each of them involved a church was a different journey. Not only did our methods for planting differ, but even the way we went about figuring out *where* to plant was unique as well.

As I shared previously, the first plant in the Southwest was heavily influenced by its proximity to family and having lived there previously. The second was seeing a brown bear in Alaska as confirmation of a calling to the Pacific Northwest. Along our journey I have met planters who planted in the same city they grew up in. They said they could not conceive of planting anywhere else, while others moved across great distances to do so. Each story is unique to the individual.

While serving as a church planting strategist I would tell potential planters that I am kind of a matchmaker. It was my responsibility to match them up with the part of the city that resonated the most with them, who they were (background, education, etc), and how God had wired them. I saw it as a combination of discerning God's call by use of a somewhat rational approach. Most often they would sense a call to move to the city to plant, if not already there; then we worked together to find a good fit for them. It was my goal to connect them with the area with which they were the most culturally compatible. Since almost all of the church planters I worked with at that time were white, then it made sense in terms of the kind of settings they ended up planting in. That was how I ended up planting where I did the first time around and yet exactly the opposite way we planted the second time.

When we moved to Metro Vancouver I was in the midst of researching and writing my dissertation, and I knew that we could not go about it the way we did it in Tucson. Instead of finding where there were the most people who were like me, I wanted to live in and plant in a diverse neighborhood that was wholly unlike me. That is why Edmonds Town Centre was a perfect fit for us. We were an ethnic and linguistic minority. We loved our community. We loved the urban culture coupled with other influences such as its cultural and socio-economic diversity, a walkable neighborhood, and accessibility to public transit.

Each planter's story is truly unique. My point here in telling my story is to simply observe that there is much to think through and process in deciding where to plant a church.

From my experience, both as a planter and a former strategist, I would argue that planters need to explore more deeply the geography of church planting. Although many church planters are indeed called to plant in a particular city, oftentimes that initial calling can be rather generic and even vague. Yet it is the first critical step that sets the planter on a certain trajectory.

My calling to the Pacific Northwest was at first rather general in nature. Over the years, it unfolded and developed. There were two aspects of this. The first is the mystical element where God prompts us to go in a certain direction. The second involves exploring and fleshing out that calling. I focused primarily on three cities; each had their own unique appeal. Portland was enticing with its vibrant downtown core and its funky neighborhoods. Seattle drew me in because I love its coffee scene and the city's "metronatural" mindset. However, Vancouver won out initially because what we really desired was diversity and an international city. Canadian cities are mind-bogglingly diverse, and Vancouver has connections globally, especially to Japan, China, southeast Asia and India.

The first part for our calling was a general sense of attraction to the Northwest. I could not shake it. I began following different news outlets and even sports teams in the region including the BC Lions, the Seattle Seahawks, the Portland Trailblazers as well the many Northwest college football teams. During the decision-making process, I was a sponge soaking it all in.

Geography is important. As a matter of fact, where we choose to live is one of the most significant decisions we can make in our lives. It affects our educational opportunities, employment possibilities, our friends, social networks, and our children's future. Place is important! It shapes everything. Church planters should carefully consider deciding where to plant knowing that the ramifications are enormous.

While some may have a generalized calling to a certain area or city, others feel led to a specific locale. Go for it. For those who are sorting through where to live in the city and plant churches, let me add the following thoughts.

One book that was pivotal in leading me to move to Vancouver was *Who's Your City?* by Richard Florida. I knew generally where God was leading us but was I was not too sure of which city or even which part of the city. I also knew that the goal was to plant in an urban setting that was culturally and ethnically diverse. When I began reading *Who's Your City?* I found myself elated and angry at the same time. I was elated because for the first time everything began coming into focus for me and angry with myself that I had not seen it earlier.

As mentioned, in the interim between Arizona and Vancouver I had taken on a ministry opportunity in the Midwest. It seemed like a logical move. The brown bear would simply have to wait. We moved there with our hearts in our stomachs. Arizona had been a great time in our lives and significant in many ways. We were hopeful and also looking forward to this next chapter. The only problem was we realized that this chapter was only the length of a paragraph.

I knew I wasn't supposed to be there. In *Who's Your City?* Florida discusses the three most important decisions we will ever make in life: *what we will do* (job, career), *with whom* (spouse), and *where*. It was the "where" that caused me anguish. I felt stuck in a small Midwestern city. That old brown bear continued to haunt me.

Florida's book was critical in finally getting me to the tipping point where I could not do anything else than go to Vancouver. "The place we choose to live affects every aspect of our being. It can determine the income we earn, the people we meet, the friends we make, the partners we choose, and the options available to our children and families."[1] As I processed Florida's three questions I began prayerfully navigating my own life and calling, and how God had wired me.

Part of Florida's book deals with the overall personality of cities. It's a unique blending of psychology and urban geography. "Are people happier when they find a community that fits them? What happens when one's personality is different from that of their community?"[2] When I read that something clicked. I began to think about and look at cities differently. They really do have a personality per se. Think of cities like Los Angeles, New York, Chicago, or Boston. Each has more than its own vibe; it has a collective personality. Again, this was one of

---

[1] Florida, *Who's Your City?* 5-6.

[2] Ibid., 190.

the reasons why Vancouver continued to rise to the top of the list for us.

Not only does each city have its own personality but so do each part of the city. Each urban neighborhood is unique and each suburb is different. Church planters who are considering where to locate in the city ought to consider this. The would-be church planter needs to painstakingly work through the where of planting, which is no small feat.

Life in Edmonds Town Centre was filled with tension, more than I could have known going in. In many ways, it was so different from who we were that after about six months, we thought we might have made a mistake. We had wanted something completely different from who we were and our neighborhood provided that. As we would venture into other parts of the city I would sometimes turn to Katie and say, "Wow, these are our people. They are just like us." In talking about it we realized how much we were indeed falling in love with our neighborhood. Some areas have that instant "fall in love factor" but for us it was slow burning and slow growing.

Site selection for church planting is not a simple process. It involves a confluence of numerous issues and factors ranging from one's upbringing, personality type, family type, education, prior work background and experience, philosophy of life, and even one's theological framework in regards to the city. If a church planter views the city in a negative light, as I used to, then it is more than likely that they will gravitate towards the suburban fringe. Cities confront our deepest biases and reveal who we really are.

This chapter exposes the deep tension that comes choosing where to plant a church. For some it is easy but for many others it is a long journey. In some instances, it is very clear not only which city to plant in but also which neighborhood or district. For the rest, these things can take a while to figure out.

The point I am attempting to make here is to stop and reconsider. The first question to ask yourself is: *Is God calling me to this part of the city?* Am I deciding based on preference or fear? Are cultural compatibility and geographic familiarity the factors that weigh the heaviest? My fear is that if we church planters only stick to the parts of the city that we like, love, and are full of people just like us, then there will be many parts of the city that will remain untouched. Is God truly calling most planters to only plant in suburban settings or in the chic urban districts?

My intent is not to argue in favor of any particular direction but rather to raise more questions for you to think through. I have experimented with creating some type of assessment tool for church planters that would open their eyes to the importance of the geography of church planting. My simple plea is for church planters to listen to God's voice and work in partnership with him to figure out the exact "where" knowing that he's created each planter and has uniquely wired them to be a good match for that part of the city where he wants them to plant their lives.

CHAPTER 4

Identity and Calling

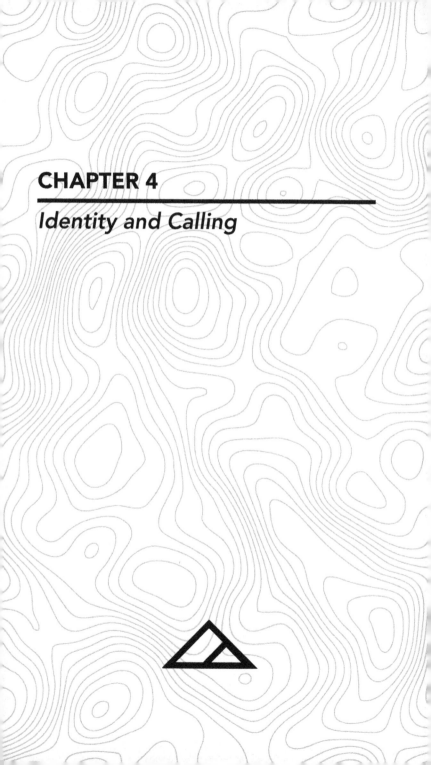

One of the foundational questions that church planters ought to ask themselves is, "How do I see myself? Am I a church planter or a missionary?" The answer will oftentimes reveal the true focus of their activities. Church planters most often would see the locus of their endeavors as starting a Christian worship gathering. The purpose of their initial funding, their end goal, would be to start some type of gathering for worship and instruction. That becomes the central focus of their energies and community: Start a church and grow it spiritually and numerically. Leaders in this category see themselves as Bible teachers, preachers, pastors/shepherds, organizers, administrators, and the like. Again, I am referring to broad and sweeping categories; I am generalizing.

Community development or engagement may or may not happen regardless of what form it takes. It may not even be on the pastor/planter's radar who instead pours most of his time and energy into developing the gathering. To be honest, this is the litmus test of how most church planters are measured by denominations, church planting networks, and donors as well how they are often evaluated. In church planting circles, those who frequently garner the most attention at conferences are those who've been successful in this pursuit. They've been able to gather a lot of people together in one place at one time. This is not a criticism but simply a reality. Those who receive funding to start churches, regardless of what they believe ought to be their priority, are ultimately measured against this rubric.

As North America's culture becomes increasingly unchurched, dechurched, or never-been-churched, the rules keep changing. Decades-old funding models, labels, and categories may now no longer apply. Today's pervasive church planter mindset might be more conducive to areas in which the majority of the population are disposed to, or grew up with, some kind of a Judeo-Christian worldview, regardless of how churched or unchurched they are. Most of them have at least a shared root memory of some sort of "God" or monotheistic deity. However, as our cities continue to swell with immigrants from countries that lack a Judeo-Christian worldview, the starting point for church planters will have to be at a much more basic level.

Much of church planting lore is about persuading the disenfranchised and the unengaged that the church is still relevant to their lives. But what does a church planter do when people aren't even disenfranchised to begin with? What if the whole idea of God, Jesus, or church is not even on their radar? While many Christians assume that is not the case in most of North America, that is simply not true.

Shortly after we moved to Canada I became aware of a college near where we lived. I had hung out long enough at a local coffee shop to see quite a number of young students reading and studying there. I began asking them where they went to school. I assumed they attended Simon Fraser University nearby. Instead, many said went to Douglas College, about a five- minute drive away.

I began learning about the college online and walking around the campus. I could not find a single campus ministry of any kind, even though the school had 7,000 to 8,000 students. When the student union confirmed to me that that in fact there were none, I asked about starting one myself. It turned out that they wanted to expand and strengthen the campus club scene, and so I was given the green light..

Sure enough, there were enough students interested and we applied for club status. I was talking with one student who was processing our club paperwork as we tried to figure how to fill in the application. She knew we were a newly forming Christian club and one of the questions on the application concerned the nature of our activities. I shrugged my shoulders and asked her what would be appropriate to put down. What she said completely shocked me: "I don't know. I really know nothing about Christianity."

Here was a student in her early 20s, tech savvy, part of the global youth culture ... who did not know anything about Christianity! It was not even on her radar. I surmised that her family had immigrated from India or possibly the Middle East and that she was typical of college-age young adults in Vancouver.

I'm convinced that in many other contexts we in North America are dealing with a culture that has been turned off by the church. But what do we do with a culture that was never turned on to it in the first place? Since they have never been franchised, they can't be seen as disenfranchised. Nor can they be seen as apathetic or disinterested, given their fundamental ignorance of Christianity.

This goes back to people's mindset—do they see themselves as a church planter or a missionary? As I track a myriad of church plants online, a common theme emerges. They are out to make church relevant, uplifting, cool, encouraging, appealing, hip, and inspiring whether through music, teaching style, or ambiance. Thousands have come to faith in Christ in such churches. Is this the same trajectory of the planters who sees themselves as missionaries?

What is the biggest difference between leaders who see themselves as missionaries whose priority is to engage the culture as opposed to those who make church planting the priority? Is there a marked distinction between beginning with community development or creating startups versus planting a church? You might think I'm splitting hairs, but I believe there is an enormous difference between being a church planter and a missionary who starts churches.

The reality is that most of our American church planting activities would not work elsewhere. No one questions that. Why? Because we understand there will be cultural differences. But are there? It's widely assumed that church planters need to do one thing here and something completely different somewhere else. That is true to the extent that it's part of being contextual. But it's not entirely true. The point I am trying to make is that North America is in fact a bona fide mission field, and therefore we need to reorient our posture as many others have recently argued. It is easy to propose these ideas when talking with other church planters, but the reality is it is much harder to implement, especially when their funding is tied to numerical expectations.

I recall having coffee with a church planter in North Vancouver. He said that out of its roughly 200,000 residents, there might be upwards of only 4,000 in church on any given Sunday. (This was about ten years ago). That's a mere two percent of the population! Which approach would have more resonance in such an environment—church planter or missionary?

How are their approaches different? Speaking only in generalities and only for the purpose of stimulating discussion, a missionary's immediate goal is often not to start a worship service but rather to enculturate themselves. They learn the local language and customs as they begin to weave their lives into the fabric of their host city and build relationships. The end goal is to proclaim the gospel, and out of that, hopefully, a church will arise. This is not church planting as we've come to know it in North America. But why should methods that are used overseas not be tried here, especially when we have a long history of exporting to other places our ways of doing church?

The simple truth is we cannot do church planting the same way we have done it even in this past decade. A new way forward is essential. Somehow there needs to be a convergence between the practices we use within our own country or region and methods we use elsewhere. This is where community development comes in. The gospel has the power to do more than fix our bad habits. The ramifications are far reaching!

The Adventure of Vocation

CHAPTER 5

Place and Calling

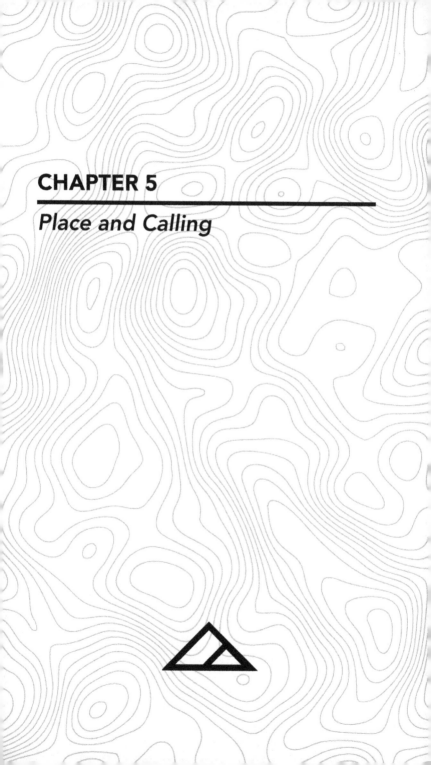

I remember telling my wife that when I turned thirty I wanted to get a head start on my midlife crisis so I could get it out of the way. I got really radical and bought a mountain bike (I actually assembled a used one with mismatched components) and several years after that I picked up a $750 moped. My midlife crisis was averted, and I moved back into the domestic duties of being a dad and breadwinner. It was a close call.

Throughout my thirties and now into my forties, I think about identity a lot. Since I'm not open enough to have these conversations with others, I end up with a continuous inner dialogue with myself, which only reinforces my insecurities. Interestingly, though, my wellbeing in terms of my identity seems to rise and fall not only with what I am doing with my life, but more importantly on *where* I live. Same guy, same everything, but labels and geography play a key role.

You might think this is shallow and self-centered thinking that only reinforces insecurity, but it is still there. While I know I am shaped by the gospel and that I am the aroma of Christ to God, I am still influenced by my environment.

Place shapes our identity. It is directly influenced and impacted by place.

When I travel, I sense a certain gravitas on my part when I say I am from Portland. People don't really know I grew up in small-town Iowa. People from Iowa are perceived a certain way, just as people from Portland are perceived a certain way. One diminishes your social standing, while the other gives you kudos.

Particularly since I'm passionate about biking, when I say "I'm from Portland," people listen. I'm the same guy I was in Iowa or Tucson, but if I tried to sell those ideas without the Portland label, I don't know that anyone would buy them.

Unfortunately, within ministry or church planting circles, the conversation is the same. As I've said more times than I can remember, all of the cool cities or cool spots in the city are on the receiving end of a glut of church planters. Yet we continue to shy away from uncool cities and uncool parts of the city. "Do you mean I should plant a church among uncool people? People who don't get my tastes in fashion, who don't get my sophisticated music tastes, who don't get my fine coffee or beer palette, or who generally don't get my chic urbanite leanings? You mean plant a church among *those kinds of people*? Those people who drink Folgers, pound Miller Lites, drive beat-up pickup trucks, shop for clothes at Walmart, listen to country music, and are not educated? Why would anyone throw their life away to plant a church in *those* cities and in *those* neighborhoods?"

If we find our identity in living in cool places, we will keep planting churches in the neighborhoods where we bump into many other cool church planters in the same coffee shop. It is not uncommon for me to hear of two, three, or four church planters *all* planting in the same cool neighborhood. While each began unaware of the others, they are planting their denominational flags in the soil of this trendy neighborhood (or one that's transitioning into a trendy district). If we want to challenge this trend of planting in trendy places, then we need to peel back the layers and get into the heart of things, namely our identity.

Identity and Calling

More honesty. Often authors write about topics that either interest them in or are wrestling with. If one were to read all my books in one sitting, there is little doubt that along with my passion for understanding the city, the shaping influence of the built environment and transportation infrastructure, and church planting in urban contexts, there are other subplots woven throughout. Calling is a topic I constantly pick up, polish for a while, and put back down.

This past week I picked up the book *Vocation: Discerning Our Callings in Life* by Douglas J. Schuurman. To say that I devoured it would be an understatement. In a matter of a few days I not only had read the book, but I had dog-eared, underlined, starred, and written on countless pages. The book jolted and jarred my thinking. Perfect timing for this chapter.

Not long ago a church planter asked me what prompted me to become an author. Ironically, I don't consider myself an author, nor do I brandish that term to identify myself. My response was probably more uninspiring than helpful. I simply replied that I write to wrestle. I write to learn. I write to hammer out intriguing (to me) concepts. I write to go deeper on topics I want to learn about. Sometimes I enter into a writing project with only vague ideas of where I want to go and no idea how to get there. That's why calling resurfaces in many of my books.

Calling is a subject that haunts me. Perhaps it haunts you, too. Not haunt in a doom-and-gloom sense, but rather in the sense that I want to make sure I'm not only living a life worth living, but doing so for the glory of God, the furtherance of the gospel, and the flourishing of humanity. I want to "get it right."

Schuurman addresses the modern assumptions about calling that are not only deceptive, but have an enormous pull and influence on the *where* of church planting. "A related modern assumption is that to have a calling is to experience self-fulfillment in that calling. A job is a way to get a paycheck, but a vocation is more than that; it is a realm of self-fulfillment."[3] When we reduce calling to a sense of self-fulfillment, why would anyone in his right mind ever think of planting a church in an uncool city or uncool neighborhood? It is to this end that Schuurman continues, "It is not fulfillment of the self but the glory of God and the welfare of the neighbor that ought to determine 'vocational' choices, insofar as there is room for choice. In and through one's vocation one picks up one's cross, follows Christ, and participates in his self-sacrificial sufferings. Christians should not aim at self-fulfillment."[4]

This is not an attempt to browbeat anyone into overlooking or neglecting how God wired us, how we grew up, the influence of our environment, our DNA, personality, or giftings. But it is an attempt to push back against an *Americanized* version of that calling that seeks self-gratification and comfort. Let's be honest.

---

[3] Schuurman, *Vocation*, 117.

[4] Ibid., 118.

Why don't church planters want to plant in unassuming neighborhoods? There are lots of reasons. Bad schools, unsightly streetscapes, too many pawnshops and check-cashing businesses, neighborhood instability, and depreciating home values. One incentive in past decades for many church planters landing in the family-friendly suburbs was good schools and family security.

I've had these kinds of conversations with a number of church planters. In their minds why would God call them to parts of the city where the schools were average or underperforming? Why would God call them to parts of the city where they may not be able to have a slice of the American dream (a single-family detached home with a big yard for the kids)? Why would God call them to the parts of the city where there are many lower-income families? Certainly, God would not call planters there. Besides, it may negatively impact their self-image as a pastor.

Admittedly I am being a little harsh. But you see, we *all* have these kinds of internal conversations. We all do. We're just too embarrassed to admit it. It's okay. I am with you. But I've also made the plunge. I did the unthinkable before my family landed in Portland. We sold our suburban home with four bedrooms and a massive two-car garage. We moved into an urban neighborhood in Vancouver, BC, where most kids didn't speak English as their first language. Out of the fifty schools in the district, ours ranked forty-seventh. Third from the bottom. We moved into a tiny apartment. We walked and used public transit exclusively.

Do you want to know what hurt the most? My identity. It messed with me. Shopping at the Dollar Tree for groceries and getting all of our clothes at the thrift store was not cool or trendy. It was hard. Yet it was what it was. We survived. We made it. We grew. We learned. We loved it. Best thing that could have happened to us. Changed everything about how I view cities, live in them, and experience them.

On the flip side I am *not* saying that everyone should go and do likewise. That would be foolish. This is descriptive and not prescriptive. My goal is not to shame you into moving to uncool cities or uncool neighborhoods. I am simply pleading with you to have an honest conversation with yourself.

The funny thing about internal dialogue is that you actually can be brutally honest. Weigh all the variables and alternatives. If you opt for the burbs or a cool gentrified neighborhood, then to God be the glory. But if you're motivated by cool, then maybe you need to hit the pause button and think things through some more.

Again, Dr. Schuurman says:

> All pivotal decisions should be shaped by a sense of calling, by our desire to express gratitude to God for the gift of salvation by using our gifts to serve others and glorify God. This includes career decisions,

decisions relating to marriage and family, decisions to join this or that church community, and various other major commitments to voluntary organizations. All of these should be motivated by *gratitude* toward God and directed by *freedom* working in love to serve God and our neighbors. The call to be a Christian must govern all decisions about callings. Pivotal decisions, like decisions within one's callings, ought to be guided by love, shaped by shalom, and tested by discernment.[5]

The goal then is that our lives become so radically shaped by the gospel and what God thinks of us that place has little bearing on our identity. Then we will discover the freedom, motivated by gratitude, to wholeheartedly love the least and the last around us.

---

[5] Ibid., 130.

The Adventure of Vocation

CHAPTER 6

*How Do I Know What I Am
Called To?*

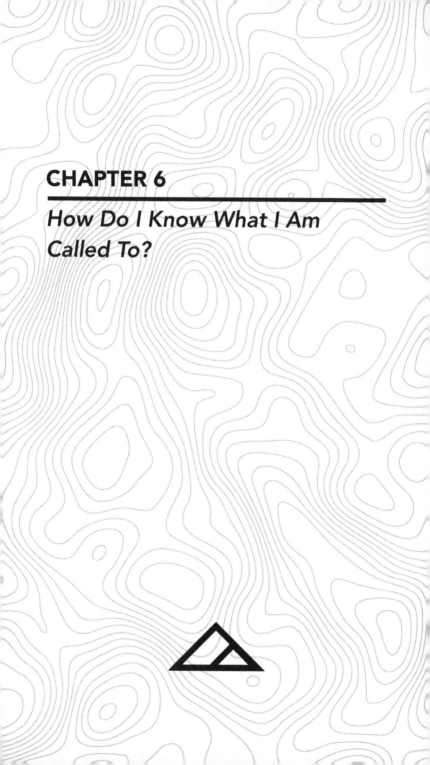

Rescuing calling and vocation from the world of professional ministry is essential. Why? Because we are participants in God's work of *shalom* in the world regardless of where our paycheck comes from. It seems ironic and profound that the Creator of the cosmos entrusts us with his work to bring about *shalom* in this world. While we're not the final act, we play a role. While the extent of our role is debatable among different groups, but nonetheless we are active participants. Our roles spill into all aspects of life, both "sacred" and "secular."

Douglas Schuurman touches on this when he writes, "If Christians are to become faithful participants in the purposes and processes of creation and redemption, it is essential that they hold together both the 'sacred' and the 'secular,' the 'religious' and 'non-religious' aspects of experience, and that they do so in a way that affirms the importance and integrity of each. This unity of life under God's reign is brought about by a vital sense of life as vocation."[6] What this means is that calling and vocation are not restricted to places and roles that are merely "religious." Whether church planting or urban planning, we all have a role to play. Calling encompasses both.

How do our sense of individual callings, what it means to be a disciple, vocation, the mission of the church, and the needs of the world intersect and overlap? John Friedmann,

---

[6] Schuurman, *Vocation*, 52.

in the introduction to his book *Insurgencies: Essays in Planning Theory*, lets the reader into his inner life. Friedmann's scholarly works and insights into planning are legendary, as he has influenced generations of urban planners. In *Insurgencies,* he uses the words "vocation" and "calling" in the same sense that pastors and missionaries do. He writes to young aspiring planners:

> In closing, then, allow me to tell you, the reader, why the idea of planning as a *vocation* still appeals to me, and why despite many setbacks, errors, and disenchantments, I nevertheless believe that planning as a field of professional study and practice is as valid a vocation as any other on the horizon. For some young people this claim may be sufficient reason to stumble into our field with an ardent desire to "do good competently" or to "change the world."[7]

---

[7] Friedmann, *Insurgencies,* 11.

Most often, and this is a tension I have lived with since becoming a Christian in college, there is a belief that *calling* or *vocation* (in the sense of divine origins) has been reserved for professional clergy, whether pastors, missionaries, or other Christian workers. It is as if those who are paid to do ministry are the only ones called, and everyone else is left to figure out careers on their own, without divine intervention. What Friedmann asserts, as an example, whether he has in mind the sense of vocation as originating in God or not, is that we are called to *be* something or to *do* something. Not only that, but he boldly writes of his career as an urban planner, whether in Chile or China or teaching at UCLA, as a *calling*. I believe that he is onto something. I would even contend that this notion of calling is not reserved for only those who identify with and follow Christ. God, in his care for creation (which includes cities) has called out many to help steward, care, lead, and influence culture as part of common grace.[8]

Michael Novak, writes in his book *Business as a Calling*, "We didn't give ourselves the personalities, talents, or longings we were born with. When we fulfill these—these gifts from beyond ourselves—it is like fulfilling something *we were meant to do.*"[9] What he wrote is pause-worthy. For many who read those words and allow them to sink in, they are a great comfort. We did not choose our personalities, nor our talents, nor our longings. This is something I have personally wrestled with over the years. We often play the comparison game, especially when we see great attributes in others that we desire. Instead, most of us need to simply learn to become more comfortable in our own skin, knowing that God has hardwired us this way ... *for a purpose.*

---

[8] Read the section entitled "Can a Calling Be Entirely Secular" in chapter 1 in *Business as Calling* by Michael Novak.

[9] Novak, *Business as Calling*, 18. Italics mine.

Those around me know I have a deep-seated passion, love, interest, fascination, and heart for cities. Having grown up in small-town Iowa, I did not come by this naturally nor early on, but somewhere along the way God supernaturally infused this love and passion within me. I did not seek this, as I used to despise cities and was terrified of them, but over time it became like a homing beacon that mysteriously altered my gravitational pull. I have concluded that involvement in cities is part of my calling. R. C. Sproul writes, "The question we as Christians wrestle with is, 'Am I in the center of God's will with respect to my vocation?' In other words, 'Am I doing with my life what God wants me to do?'" [10]

Sproul and Novak both offer thoughts that are helpful as we consider what we are called to as disciples in cities. Again, do not narrowly define this conversation only to those who are in paid professional ministry. Sproul sets out

---

[10] Sproul, *Can I Know God's Will?*, Loc. 453.

four questions to think through: "The problem with discerning one's calling focuses heavily on four important questions:

- What *can* I do?
- What do I *like* to do?
- What would I like to be *able* to do?
- What *should* I do?

The last question can plague the sensitive conscience."[11] As we look at the work before us as Christ's diplomats, ambassadors, and missionaries to our communities, these questions help form the shape of our calling. Pastors are not the only ones needing to answer these questions, and as Friedmann articulated, people in non-clergy occupations

---

[11] Ibid., Loc. 474.

can have an equal sense of *calling* and *vocation.*[12]

Novak says, "To identify [callings], two things are normally required: the God-given ability to do the job and the (equally God-given) enjoyment in doing it because of your desire to do it."[13] In *Business as a Calling*, Novak spells out four characteristics of calling:

- First, each calling is unique to each individual. Each of us is as unique in our calling as we are in being made in the image of God.
- Second, a calling requires certain preconditions. It requires more than desires; it requires talent. For a calling to be right, it must fit our abilities.
- Third, a true calling reveals its presence by the enjoyment and sense of renewed

---

[12] I am reminded of a recent conversation with a friend who is a transportation planner working for the city. Having grown up as a pastor's kid, he knows what ministry as a career and calling is all about. For a while, he wrestled with whether God was calling him in this direction. Instead, he sensed God was leading him down the path that he is on now as a planner. He would describe his job in terms of *calling* and *vocation*.

[13] *Business as Calling*, 19.

energies its practice yields us. Enjoying what we do is not always a feeling of enjoyment; it is sometimes the gritty resolution a man or woman shows in doing what must be done—perhaps with inner dread and yet without whimpering self-pity.

- A fourth truth about callings is also apparent; they are not usually easy to discover. Frequently many false paths are taken before the satisfying path is last uncovered. Experiments, painful setbacks, false hopes, discernment, prayer, and much patience are often required before the light goes on.[14]

At times, this calling may propel us in the direction of seeking common grace in the city, while at other times, we are called to focus more on the saving grace aspects. These are not mutually exclusive because an urban planner, while seeking the peace and welfare of the city through equitable planning also lives as a missionary, diplomat, and ambassador of the King. Conversely, those more focused on

---

[14] Ibid., 34-35.

saving grace in terms of their calling can also lean into gospel demonstration as well. In other words, regardless of where and how we lean in light of our callings, vocations, and occupations, it does not mean we should neglect common or saving grace.

Os Guinness in *The Call* writes, "God normally calls us along the lines of our giftedness, but the purposes of giftedness are stewardship and service, not selfishness. Giftedness does not stand alone in helping us discern our callings. It lines up in response to God's call alongside other factors, such as family heritage, our own life opportunities, God's guidance, and our unquestioning readiness to do what he shows."[15] Guinness builds on this and contends that calling should precede what jobs we take, which then helps guides us in our decision-making process. "A sense of calling should precede a choice of job and career, and the main way to discover

---

[15] Guinness, *The Call*, 45.

calling is along the line of what we are each created and gifted to be. Instead of 'You are what you do,' calling says: 'Do what you are'" [16]

What does this have to do with the mission of the church and our role in the communities we live in? This can be answered in numerous ways from the corporate, institutional, or organizational church to individual Christians. This conversation of calling also affects the spread of new churches in our communities and where and why new churches are being planted where they are.

But more than that, this conversation on calling opens up the topic of how churches are to approach their communities. What should their responses be? How should the church engage, both individually as Christians and corporately as a body, in the city? How does a sense of calling shape the mission of the church?

---

[16] Ibid.

These questions radiate from our notions of calling, the mission of the church, and common and saving grace. The church, since its inception in the first century, has always been about extending both arms of grace to the watching world. At times, we have done remarkably well and at other times we have failed miserably, but I believe the impetus comes from this sense of mission and calling to be salt and light to the world. As a result, we are compelled to do something about human suffering, we respond in the face of global and local calamities, and have a history of setting up schools (from elementary schools to universities), orphanages, and hospitals. If our primary mission were to simply be about evangelism and discipleship, then many of these society-shaping institutions would never have been birthed.

The point in this conversation of calling and vocation is we get to think through *where* and *how* we live these out. For some it may be in paid professional ministry roles. Even within that category there's an enormous diversity of what that looks like ... pastor, church planter, medical missionary, community developer, educator, prison chaplain, CEO of a faith-based international development organization, professor, and everything in between. For others it is an equally called career of a medical practitioner, immigration lawyer, architect, gym instructor, break dancer, school teacher, and so much more. The less we get caught up on titles and labels the more we'll be free to live into our callings and vocation.

That is where we'll land this conversation: Freedom. Freedom to drop labels. Freedom to be who God made you to be. Freedom to be drawn towards what you love and are passionate about. Freedom to live our lives for the benefit of others. Calling and vocation are not gifts that we hoard. They are God-given gifts and leanings for the betterment of our world and the furtherance of the gospel.

The Adventure of Vocation

CHAPTER 7

How Do I Know What To Start?

The question on the minds of a lot of people who begin orbiting the Intrepid world, is "what do I even start?" It comes up often in our cohorts. With seemingly a million ideas and options on the table the prospect can be daunting. It's akin to being a high school senior and still fretting over which college to attend as well as which degree program to pursue. For most that truly is daunting.

Maybe it was because I was that high schooler. Not sure what to study or where. Sure, I had ideas and an inclination but I was almost paralyzed with indecision. Fast forward nearly 30 years. These days I spend time in the classroom each and every semester helping college students process these same kinds of decisions. Looking back on my high school self what I realized is this ... *I actually knew what I wanted to do with my life.*

Did I have specifics? No. Details? Not a bit. But I did have an inclination and a leaning. There was this compulsion to gravitate in a certain direction. I had a trajectory. Ironically, this was even before I came to faith in Christ. As a result, when Christ called me to himself and into a life of service to him, it didn't involve a break from who I was, how I was wired, but rather a deeper leaning into that direction.

I'm finally comfortable saying I'm a creative person. I'm curious. I like creating things from scratch. Whereas I once thought that meant going to art school and pursuing the creative arts, I instead have applied those leanings to ministry, from church planting to starting ministries and projects, to writing books and starting new businesses. In other words, I didn't have to stop being me to become what God formed me to be.

Knowing what to start as far as a business or non-profit is concerned is similar to this very conversation. We simply gravitate towards certain things and away from others. It's like food. For some reason I love asparagus but hate (and I mean hate) cauliflower. Why? I have no idea. No matter how much I try I cannot bring myself to enjoy that abomination. But asparagus? Love it. Who knows why we love certain things and avoid others? We do this in life and we do it when it comes to starting a new business or non-profit.

Many of you may feel like that high schooler sitting with the guidance counselor thumbing through the catalog (or perusing websites) of college options and degree programs. Overwhelmed. I'd like to encourage you that you're actually closer to your vocation and calling than you realize. More than likely you're already trending in the direction you need to go in, but you're hesitant. Maybe afraid. *"You mean, start that? No way. I can't do that."* But you actually can. You will acquire skills and tools needed along the way. Trust me.

So how do you know what to start? I'm sure you don't realize that you already have a list of three or more possible options. How did you come up with that list? It might've been from an experience, a passion, an interest. I also suspect with within that list there are one or two that resonate even more deeply. They stir you more than the others. Again, it's not always easily explainable … you just know.

So then, the question is … how do you go from idea to startup? To me the biggest and most difficult decision is landing on an idea. Once you get going, of course, you're going to realize just how much you don't know, but we learn, adapt, and accumulate skills and tools along the way.

Current needs + Who You are + Missio Dei = New Startup Venture

Overlooked in so much of the conversation surrounding church planting as well as startups is this simple admonition and encouragement: *be yourself!* I know, shocking. At Intrepid I like to ask the following questions:

- What if church planting was actually simple and freeing?
- What if you could actually bring your passions and skills into ministry?
- What would it look like to plant churches *here* as we do *over there?*
- What if church planting and launching startups meant simply *being you?*

The same goals and aspirations apply to both church planting, launching a startup, or a community economic development. In all of them, the clincher is you can actually be yourself. No cookie-cutter approach here. No listening to all the assessment results which try to pigeon-hole you into a certain expression of church or startup. The truth is we're like snowflakes ... we're all unique. There is no one else like us. Even those most like us are really nothing like us.

I was reminded of this during a luncheon a couple days ago for faculty who teach in the Masters of Global Development and Justice program at Multnomah University. Sitting around a table as we feasted on foods from Venezuela and Mexico, the conversation turned towards Enneagram and personality types. Even when it came to the Myers-Briggs personality test, it wasn't surprising to me that most of us had nearly identical results. My hunch is academia attracts certain kinds of people. But the truth is we couldn't be more wonderfully different from one another.

We all grew up in different parts of the country and the world, had disparate experiences growing up, and in adulthood, have found divergent interests, hobbies, and so forth. Even though we all share in common a deep interest in justice and international development, each of us tackle this conversation differently. We each address these topics from our unique perspectives based upon our experiences, interests, and personalities.

Why then should we assume that we all should plant churches and launch startups the same way? And yet so much of our training, assessment metrics, and funnels seem more about cranking out uniform widgets than working with individuals to hone what and where they *should* start.

Seemingly every church planter I come across is planting the same way as the next planter. All of their social media looks the same. What they take photos of, the presets and filters they use, the logos, wording, and so on ... all look the same. It's like the Third Wave coffee scene. It doesn't matter what city I'm in, they all look the same. Same decor ... color palette, succulent plants, wood highlights, claims, and more. Where have creativity and innovation gone?

I'm not saying this is wrong or bad or anything like that when it comes to launching coffee shops. But they seem to be on a similar trajectory as church planting. Uniformity. But here's the good news: they all don't have to fit this cookie-cutter approach.

What if church planters and entrepreneurs felt the freedom to be themselves? Start according to *their* timelines. To look how *they* want to. Engage in a process that resonates with *their* personality, gifting, perspective, experiences, and context. And fit into and resonate with *their* unique context.

This is why I love this simple equation: *current needs + who you are + missio Dei = new startup venture.* That's simple math. I like simple math.

What does your community need? Not every community needs a new hip Third Wave coffee shop. It could be a welding company, auto body shop, barber shop, daycare, or a tech company that helps farmers utilize drones with an app on their phones. The possibilities are endless. The needs in your community are all around you. But then we need to match this need with who you are.

I'm not sure I'm qualified to do any of the things listed in the previous paragraph. Do you *really* want me to cut your hair? (I have a weed whacker I can use.) I personally wouldn't pursue any of those. I'd keep digging to uncover something that resonates with who I am, my background, experiences, passions, interests, and leanings. It's as simple as that. Besides, why would I want to start something that doesn't light my fire? It's already challenging enough to bring something to life from scratch. We need that fire to keep us going when we're in the midst of the monotony and grind of planting and startups.

Next, we look at the narrative that's throughout Scripture of God's redemptive plan. History is a timeline of what God is doing in the world. *Shalom* was lost in Eden. As a result, we're to be about bringing and extending this *shalom* wherever we go and in whatever we do.

This is where we extend both God's saving and common grace to our communities. Embodying and sharing the gospel. How is your startup and church bringing about healing, restoration, and health to our communities?

All of these questions and thought processes can lead us towards starting something that truly resonates with who we are as well as meeting a need or filling a niche in our community. There is great freedom here. Maybe so much freedom that it causes us fear, apprehension, and even paralysis. But as I've said before, we all have interests and leanings. We probably even have a few ideas that keep bubbling up to the surface.

It's time to run up our sails and catch the wind. The biggest step is the first step. Step onto the boat. Hoist your sails. Head out of the safe harbor.

Bibliography

Florida, Richard. *Who's Your City? How the Creative Economy Is Making Where to Live the Most Important Decision of Your Life.* New York: Basic, 2008.

Friedmann, John. *Insurgencies: Essays in Planning Theory.* New York: Routledge, 2011.

Guiness, Os. *The Call: Finding and Fulfilling the Central Purpose of Your Life.* Nashville: W Publishing, 2003.

Novak, Michael. *Business as Calling: Work and the Examined Life.* New York: The Free Press, 1996.

Schuurman, Douglas. J. *Vocation: Discerning Our Callings in Life.* Grand Rapids: Wm. B. Eerdmans, 2004.

Sproul, R.C. *Can I Know God's Will?* Orlando: Reformation Trust, 2009.

About the Author

Sean Benesh lives in the Pacific Northwest and is a professor, author, coffee roaster, and leads an initiative called Intrepid for The Table Network.

www.seanbenesh.com
@seanbenesh

Made in the USA
Las Vegas, NV
18 August 2021